Biography

Dileep Mani is from Kottayam, Kerala. He joined VSO Uganda in order to lead the roll out of a literacy and numeracy programme aimed at out of school youth as part of a livelihood intervention in northern Uganda. He worked in Maldives, and currently he is in India. He has published blogs and e -novel Hobo and Angel and "Hotel management training"

The poem is about praising Lord Shiva and Devi and describing their physical forms. The mantras basically praise the Gods and when you please the Gods with an intention t is ful filled. Island belle is a romantic love poem

 Between my body and your body and Dancing Venus are romantic poems with a metaphysical touchThe poems depicts the epitome of love.

Ardhanareeshwara

The forest was green with bushes and trees.

Gazed at the hunter God with the whitest teeth.

Crescent embellished his forehead ,

Ganga fell from his dreadlocks

The famous third eye which burned the Lord of lust to ashes was retired,

Sun and moon manifested in his eyes;

Nose was chiselled and pointed,

Ears and arms were beautified with golden ear rings and bracelet,

The whitest teeth displayed a cosmic laughter.

Bluish neck which carried the hemlock of the world;

was adorned with a snake garland.

The strong four arms carried:

Axe, deer and weapons

The stomach resembled a banyan leaf

The tiger skin covered his waist

The immortal yogi who could recite stories ,

could dance in rounds which resembles the endless cycle of life and death.

lord of the three world's had his better half parvati ;

Offspring of the Vindhya mountains who bring eternal bliss

Better half of the Lord of the spirits

And destroyer of demons

Beautiful braids of hair adorn her crown

She pleases Shiva and protects the three worlds

Daughter of the ocean she washes away ego and sins

She pleases the Lord with her dance movements and offers him the eternal bliss of joy

She has the complexion of a lotus flower

Princess of love who can evoke the love in celestial beauties with dazzling teeth

Beauty of the moon is reflected on her face

Her spotless forehead and pointed nose makes the flowers sweat

The moon beams emitted from her golden yellow cloth tide to your waist is a
magnificent site for the Lord's gaze

The bosom shines like golden mountains

And her lotuses like feet are a feast to the eye

offspring of the Vindhya mountains who bring eternal bliss

Better half of the Lord of the spirits

and destroyer of demons

Beautiful braids of hair adorn your crown

you pleased Shiva and protects the three worlds

Daughter of the ocean you wash away ego and sins

you pleased the Lord with your dance movements and offered him the eternal bliss of joy

you have the complexion of a lotus flower

princess of love who can evoke the love in celestial beauties with dazzling teeth

Beauty of the moon is reflected on your face

your spotless forehead and pointed nose makes the flowers sweat

the moon beams emitted from your golden yellow cloth tide to your waist is a magnificent site for the Lord's gaze

The bosom shine like golden mountains

And the lotus like feet are a feast to the eye

The island belle with pearly fish eyes

you gazed at me I gazed at you and

our paths diverged while talking

we got lost while walking

Never once you said you love me

We never realized that the moon and star could be just friends

Mars and Venus could engage in a talk and not just a criminal conversation.

The island belle

The island belle with pearly fish eyes

you gazed at me I gazed at you and

our paths diverged while talking

we got lost while walking

You were necessary for me,

like air for breathing,

I searched for you

like feet trying to land on earth.

And then we realised the marriage vows

doesn't permit our rendevouz forever

The island belle with pearly fish eyes

you gazed at me I gazed at you and

our paths diverged while talking

we got lost while walking

I remember the sandy beaches

the uninhabited island and the

coral forest

We were in shallow water which covered our waists

I remember the soft touch

and saw a rabbit finding its burrough

it was bliss ,the smiling sun

the calming breeze and the splash of

water;

when we became one

The island belle with pearly fish eyes

you gazed at me I gazed at you and

our paths diverged while talking

we got lost while walking

since you have met me,

I felt more golden,

I don't smile just with my lips,

but with my entire body.

my days and nights were beautiful,

all this is because of you

this companionship was not there forever,

I realized when you vanished to oblivion

but when you think of me

I wish i could churn the ocean like a whirl wind and come.

The island belle with pearly fish eyes

you gazed at me I gazed at you and

our paths diverged while talking

we got lost while walking

SHE LAUGHEDShe laughed;And the shadows of me fell apart in our hands.Like threads that bound the world together ,Slipping free to become again the whole cosmos.Mountains fell into the sky,And the sky became empty and fullled.All the prophecies that came from the heart of the mountains .She laughed and the rivers turned again to silence.The rocks cried out remembering their names And the trees walked to the ends ofThe earth becoming ecstasy;In the eyes of the #owers.Sky was the mirror of in▯nity.She laughed.And the oceans fell into the sky .Where we laughed falling apart coming together

The Lord of illusion came to me.

He found me in an ocean of tears,

His laughter was the Lightning

Which struck me, spit me open

Upon the shore of consciousness.

The Lord of illusion came to me.

He smiled through the oceans of tears

To meet me laughing

On the edge of consciousness.

He devoted himself to crossing over

All of my illusions.

The Lord of illusion came to me.

He smiled as I devoted myself

To crossing over these oceans,

Desiring to leave all illusions.

Over oceans of time I crossed

To become this highest love,

Abandoning all dharmas.

2.

On the path I saw flowers laughing,

Turning in the wind as the sea rose

To carry breezes tickling dreadlocks.

From the deep seas belly I saw

An infinity of stones all alive,

Making music out of mysteries.

From the shore I touched that voice

Turning all to wonder

Like an infinity of stars laughing

In the sands beneath me.

In the path I saw flowers laughing,

Holding crystal dewdrops to my eyes

Tears of honey brimming to the brim

Of the empty mind brimming fullness.

From the deep seas belly I turned

Touching rock beneath an infinity of stones,

Swimming up from light to light

Locks bound in the music out of mystery.

On the path I saw flowers laughing

On winds flying pathless,

Turning my eyes from dreams

To this infinity laughing within me.

From the shore I touched this infinity of stones

Awakening music out of mystery.

3.

Drawing shapes in the sand

I turned being upon being

In the endless worlds knowing,

Figments of the mind touching

To touch this always going,

This ever coming back.

Drawing shapes in the sand

I turned dream upon dreaming,

Saw the end of my seeing

In the shape of my hands.

Castles were floating

On the winds sudden going,

Emptiness spilling out

Oceans of land.

Drawing shapes in the sand

I turned words upon meaning,

Where meaning became more

Than words could withstand.

So I looked past the words

To touch past the meanings

Into places where the mind

Could not sit, rise, or stand.

Where the mind was no more

There the world touched meaning,

Like a face in the dark

Burning shapes in the sand.

Drawing shapes in the sand

I turned sleep upon sleeping,

Where the forms came apart

In the seams of my hands.

There the seeds of the past

And the future of being,

Awoke like a glass

Slipping out of my hands.

I awoke like a glass

Slipping sleep into seeing,

Sands upon sands

In the shapes in my hands.

4.

The rain is falling, turning arrows into flowers

At the edge of night, where the voices

Of the moon gather in your palms,

Spilling across my eyes like a sea of stars.

The rain is falling, sharpening swords

On the edge of night, where the wind wakes

Inside your dreaming a sea of flowers,

Voices of the moon spill over.

The rain is falling, touching hidden fire

That burns through the voices in our wounds,

Bleeding on the edge of night

Turning arrows into flowers.

The rain is falling, washing us ashore

To where we lift the edge of night,

Peeling open lids to light

Flooding the seas of flowers.

5.

A man goes and takes his seat in the chair.

A woman rolls out a mat on the ground and kneels.

Greetings begin like a sweet chorus rising

To gradually dissolve in the murmurs

Melting behind pursed lips.

A man speaks from his seat on the chair.

A woman nods from within lowered eyes,

Her eyes rising to meet his eyes

Like the breeze scattering flowers.

A man turns in his seat on the chair.

A woman watches holding silence,

Cutting the stems from greens

Sorting leaves from her seat on the mat

Where she kneels.

A man becomes still in his seat on the chair.

A woman turns words over like the leaves

In her hands that move towards silence,

Gathering to touch in the clear air.

A man nods from his seat on the chair.

A woman shapes the form of his nodding,

Unknowingly he is turned and woven

Like the threads woven and bound

In the mat on which she kneels.

A man rises to stand from his seat on the chair.

A woman looks up from sorting leaves,

To sift through voices rising in a chorus

Ascending to descend in murmurs.

A man walks away from his seat on the chair.

A woman remains seated behind,

Sorting leaves in the cool of the emptiness

That scatters flowers on the air.

6.

Bound by the secrets of the stars

I follow your eyes unbinding,

Where you drink the knowledge

Of yourself in my eyes.

In the secrets of the stars

I touch a single thread unwinding,

Where you drink the nectar of webs

Dissolving in my eyes.

Bound in the fire of the stars

I follow this path of abiding,

In the joy that rushes through rivers

And rests in the deep of your eyes,

Where you drink of the stillness shining

Alive in the space of divining,

Where stars fall awake in our eyes.

7.

Climbing into the heart of the sacred mountain,

The wind carried away leaves on my breath

Far away down the long rivers flowing

Into the valley of flowers, where time measured

Stillness and light upon the eternal ache and magic

Of an always waking childhood.

Climbing into the heart of the sacred mountain,

The stones under my feet turned

Revealing beneath the humility of dust

The endless faces of adoration shining

A harvesting of gold.

Climbing into the heart of the sacred mountain

I walked in the footsteps of my kind mothers,

Following the clear green to the voice of streams

Where I drank deep after deep

The nectar of love's bestowing.

Climbing into the heart of the sacred mountain,

I saw thoughts dissolve into the sky

Like dewdrops on the petals of flowers

Melting away on the winds of dawn,

Where I walk dreaming awake

Towards flight that reaches the thoughtless.

The days pass unconscious of themselves. Who are we, that exist, knowing? What separates us from the days, which hold no pain or memory? No good or evil? Without desires, without thoughts, the days simply go on and on, endlessly, beautifully, perfectly mindless.

2. I cannot hold you any longer. You slip from my heart seamlessly. I open my eyes, I scan everything before me, I breathe more slowly than ever before, but I cannot find you now. My self is slipping away. The elements take me, I am not my own. My will is shattered, hauled and tossed to and fro on the waves of a greater being. I falter, I touch ground. The universe swallows me and spits me back up. I am a home and I am a stranger in that home. There is no ground to hold you on, only the love that a stranger has for a strange thing which he cannot understand

3. In this desire, I am emptied of all words. I am suddenly nothing. I am completely silent, I am puddy in the hands of the universe. I want to make love, I want to cry, I want to break into a million pieces, I want to run screaming, all at once. But I do nothing. I do not move, sitting perfectly still, I wait.

4. The answer lies in the pain. If I cannot speak, then I should be silent. If I cannot be silent, then I should freely speak. Is there is grief, I must speak to it. If there is shame, I must accept it. Where there is love, I must move in its direction. If I am bitter, I must go and unearth the root from which it festers. If I know something, I will be able to act. If I act, I will change.

5. You are young. You are thrown about by desire. You are being cleaved by the world, by each being that enters your world. You will grow old. You will learn to accept what cleaves you. And when you have finally surrendered all of yourself and accepted all, you will have mastered what cleaves you.

6. How will I charge my life with the power of words, if I have not become acquainted with silence?

7. Answers. Answers are the questions that choose to live. Answers are living vicariously.

8. If you touch me, will I burn? Or plunge into icebound prisons? Will I go splintering into a million fragments? Or join myself, whole, to the universe? There is no separation, only our separate wanting, our separate desires. If we can let go of these desires, we will remember our oneness.

9. Years begin to unravel, I am tracing back the threads of my life,

   Tunnels intersecting towards a harvesting of gold.

   Colours begin to astound me, textures drink at my soul.

   So many things that I thought lost, I see now

   Springing from Earth and sky, old, new, new, old.

10. I have time, time for thoughts to crawl and thoughts to fly,

    The wind and the waves tear through my mind, past time.

    I have time, time for silence and time for song,

    Time to wander, and time to belong.

    There is time for all the questions that grasp at my heart,

    Waiting unanswered in the longing and the dark.

    Opening now into light, rivers flow from my feet,

    And I start, I am far, I am far.

There is time, time enough for you, and for me,

Time enough to worship and to see,

Without wanting, without grasping higher.

There is time, time enough to hide and time to be free,

Time to act, and time to dream,

Time to let things rest and be.

I want to let things rest and be, to let them breathe,

Untouched by my own wantings, my longings,

My hauntings, my unresolved complexities,

Anxieties, my false sobriety. I want to let life come to me,

Not to chase it, nor hasten to attain it.

I want to be simplicity, purity, surrendering all the rest

To destiny. To be untaken by the myriads of trials

That fling their hooks at me, that catch me on the trail

Of an emotion. I want to learn of true devotion,

Of souls unbroken by the emptiness of words,

By the world that quickly turns and takes them.

11.To my Father

Words fall like bludgeons upon gentler ears,

Words caught thick in the venom of anger,

Words drowning in the unbounded and unseen sadness.

Your clanging cymbals beat me, caved my heart into silence,

Battered blushing youth into the corners of many storied houses,

Into the darkness of endless corridors leading further

Into sorrow and shame, where I hid from your words.

12. I always want to write you a letter, but I cannot.

I have no words to say. You ate up all my words

With your anger, you drowned so much beauty in your wrath.

And I have walked so far since, but still I have no words to say to you.

There is only barrenness in your memory, lingering sadness

And a stain.

13. In my unmade life, I am coming forth from silence. I am breathing courage

And I am not afraid. I follow the pull of the currents, no longer drowning in

Them. I am a woman extending love and grace to everyone. I am not

Withdrawn, instead I draw out. And I am no longer sneaking out windows.

14. Things to remember: you need to always be creating. Always speak the truth. Always be humble and the sadness will be gone. Avoid conflict, but you also must speak. You must always be active, things will only come to you by your seeking them out and acting. There is no room in this life for crybabies, there is no room to stay in your sorrows. You have to be a warrior, you have to keep on moving no matter what. It is the only way to live.

15. I raise an empty glass to my lips and it fills,

Wine flowing over so many barren things.

I let the dreams go, figures whom death made giant

Wane back into the everyday, into the subtle motions

Of the escaping and inarticulate.

16. Love keeps climbing higher and higher, in its presence the questions

Drop away, forgetting their own existence. Remembrance awakens

Outside of time, gathering me back to the source.

17. I cannot wait, I cannot sit silent any more, while they all go on talking,

Talking away all the days and nights. I wonder, where do they find

Their words? Where do they come from, and where are they going?

Are they the whim of each passing moment? Are they the breaths of God,

Clouded as we witness them rising? Are they our children, going ahead

Of us to inherit horizons? How much weight have they been allotted

To carry? How much of time have they spoken for?

18. I want my heart to open to all of the world, to leave nothing out. Give me patience in this. Something in my self runs ahead of me, leaving this body behind, wandering and struggling against struggles.

There are no secrets in love. How long have I been hiding in secrets? There is no mystery except for the unfolding of the present moment, everything that is, already lives in the universe.

You taught me how to dream. And in the chaos of our dreams we began to unlearn everything, seeing the birth of the world in our own selves. Becoming one, we saw what it was to be separate, we began to understand the force that drives apart and unites one to the other. I began to see that there is no separation, only the loneliness that we feel in the belief of our being something separate.

19. The wind goes dying on your lips, and I shutter from ecstasy into silence,

A silence that tears, that breaks open to flood incalculable empty spaces,

A million visions touch my mind and vanish on the point of becoming.

I am found, and lost again in this silence, borne away on the wings

Of something older than memory, more remote than any place.

I have gone where I cannot go, and I have come back,

Back to this body, back to this hunger, back to you.

Where do I go now? Where do I begin...

To reclaim what I long to be freed from?

20. Mornings wings open over emptied shores, and I begin again to breathe.

Half lives fall away, their weight distinguished by the distance.

The madness of dread and desire have struggled to a summit within me,

Amongst the peaks of that place I hunt for you, drifting worlds away

Lost in the songs that break between us, where I search for my heart

Locked somewhere amongst stones, where the sea breaks endlessly.

21. I choose peace over comfort.

I choose love over sentiment.

I choose ecstasy over happiness.

22. White shores stand ready, still and Virgin mirrors that marry the sky.

Nothing can touch them. The night drops her hands,

full as an unsung prayer waiting suspended over the still black waters.

The journey to no place begins here, in the silence that seeks to touch God.

23. Your silence fills me, a long melody emptying twilight upon my closing eyes,

    Into my opened heart. Longing to speak unspeakable things,

    My voice slips, perishing into a multitude of dreams.

24. 1) Leaving home, the heart stumbles through thickening air,

    Making for the open skies dreaming. Fleeing the toxic tide of a worn out life,

    It breaks to shed new light.

    2) I wake in the mouth of dawn, nightmares rolling back as your breath

       carries me on in the gentlest song, baring me to myself.

       I am coming to know the unsung places I shrunk from in my past.

    3) Who are we in this maze of myriad faces? Who are we, when we choose

       To be what we thought of becoming?

    4) I remember you in the surges of an old sorrow, your weight falls back to haunt

       This shadow of a love, to touch me as I slip into dangerous beginnings.

       So many things are turning, sinking, deepening within me,

       I fight the changing light till at last my eyes succumb,

       Blinking brighter on the brush of a vision.

    5) There are none I can claim as my own. Nor can I claim myself,

       In this procession of loves that have made me.

Treasures are being lost to be found again. The sea is unending,

Like the soul it brings me back to myself, again and again.

6) Each day I can rise, I will rise to inherit the full measure of my blessings.

All of you who have broken me, have saved me,

Teaching me to love as you fashioned my soul.

When the tides turn, I will turn with them, knowing that you God, are all,

And I have no need to fear this beginning, or that ending.

7) Towards the One, I dance, these limbs lost in the festival of memory.

In the gathering of love, minds fly, freed from time and the bindings of secrets.

25. I only fear that our lives will be spent, used up in the constant exchanges

Which lead back to sorrows and confusions. That as we come together,

We will give what should not be given, and take what should not be taken,

And thus, remain alone until the end of our days.

Let us always conceive of no ending, our home beyond place

Where love always waits, opening on us the endless faces of God.

26. I am still. Let my will echo your will. In your stillness, I find me.

In my stillness, you are there, white light burning through

The dense dark of my dreaming.

27. I need to be careful not to forget why I am here. Why am I here? I am not here to

remain stuck in some past. I am not here to spend myself in chasing or changing things or people. I am not here to merely daydream. I am not here to sit and remain content, or complacent to circumstances. I am not here to perpetuate old cycles of sorrow and self pity. I am here to taste and to see, and to know everything that finds me, without carelessness and without regret. I am here to learn how to move through all things that bound me, that bind me still, to move through and beyond all these things. I am here to master myself, in order to love with more fire, more sincerity, more truth. I am here to become one with myself, with God, so that I will never be in need of anything that the world will try and buy me away with.

28. Storm

    This rain sounds me back to myself, the unsent songs of my soul fly,

    Unseated in the sparks of light that burn through our sadness.

29. You stand at the edge of the sea, wind breaking the mirrors that flashed

    Between us. You shout, one chord stretching solitary across the expanse

    Of hidden faces, one sound dispelling the years of silence, the penance of time.

    All the long nights of our fiction cease their stammering, and sink

    Beaming towards one great light, into which the mouths of the waves

    Pour praise endlessly. Our hunger is no less than that of these waves,

    No less than that thirst for the infinite, no less than the flight of extinction

    In which love merges, ending all sadness.

30. I feel the force of the ocean enter us, something insatiable

    That will not let us go uncompleted. We've been caught in the grasp

    Of our own wills, trained so long to shrink back from what we know,

    Conditioned to falter. Now we are entering a mind wholly new,

Untouched, we are carving faces into what we thought untouchable.

31. The sun drops like a coin between my hands, and I fall

    Headlong into the light that consumes. All around me the dark

    Is sinking deeper and deeper, within me the light is burning

    Brighter and brighter. The shadow of my self amasses shadows,

    These shadows amass shadows, and I watch them flee,

    Empty dreams that finally abandon themselves for the dawn.

32. The days empty themselves as fires dwindle to quiet cessation,

    Songs sinking into a ceremonious stillness.

    Spirals of smoke slip sleepily upwards from the coals,

    Seamlessly sewn to the cadence of this dance.

    The air burns with forgotten dreams, half remembered,

    Then quickly sent spinning back to space resounding.

33. A shadow falls across the page, obscuring thought from vision.

    Sorrow draws long lines through the undreamt white,

    Thickening like an iron fisted memory.

    The hinges of mind turn slowly, slowly gathering.

34. The waning light draws dreams through the air,

    Threads of the gathering hours are crossing to weave

    Their salutary silence. The oncoming night slips like

A cloud between my fingers, a wings brief eternity

Flapping in the wind.

The trappings of each day sink back to sleep

Until tomorrow resurrects them.

In this moment I sense I am an infinitude of things,

Of beings, Of many lives lived and unlived,

People spoken and unspoken.

35. Above all else, you've got to respect yourself.

   Can't love this world till you cast away the shame,

   Put to rest the blame. Won't know real peace

   Till you laugh away the past, smiles break the demons grasp.

   Can't start to dream till you open up the sea to mend

   Your sufferings. Can't see the wonders that could be

   Till you drop your vanity, the self's insanity.

   Above all else, you've got to love yourself.

   Can't know your neighbour till you know yourself,

   Can't be a lover till you own yourself.

   Can't join the rest till you can stand yourself,

   Alone and brightly shining.

36. Happenings simmer, dusk settling like an old embrace

   Over all the comings and goings,the unresolved days and

   The madness of nights coalesce, collapsing into a quiet simplicity.

All the things I held fast fall from my hands, cracking open

To spill prayers lie streamers that plume the sky.

In the lengthening shadows the streets begin to wane,

Growing distant, minute, yet closer, they pass through me

Like dreams at dawn, or water.

The voices of the dispersed crowd echoes my own lost voice

Back to me, in the vague shouts that drift out from emptying lots

And closing shops, I hear my own cry, stifled,

Then broken free into the oncoming night.

37. The eyes of all the people I meet are intersecting,

Like a great cloud in the midst of drought that heralds rain.

Each day their silent prayers and strivings flood me,

These multitudes that I love but cannot see.

Their stories stir in my blood a ceaseless invention,

An attempt to translate these places in time back to the eternal.

I pick up the pieces of old lives and begin mending,

My work is just beginning.

38. I meet you here in this silence.

I have come from far away to be heard,

To find that the only thing left to do is listen.

The ache of so many longing years has burned through

The eyes to my soul, undefinable beauty has tossed me

Like something lost to the sea. In its irrevocable cry,

I come back to what I know.

39. Your voice is a dark river through which I tread in endless adoration.

   Where can I find myself now, lost in the intonations of love?

   With each rise and fall the syllables reincarnate, and I with them.

   With each push and pulse the secrets empty out,

   Streaming towards the sea, where all things less than love will perish.

40. Your voice rings, a dream resurrecting to shatter a still life into motion.

   High on the summit the wind cries with gathering insistence,

   Tearing from me this burden to become, to know what I cannot know,

   To possess all that I have known.

   The night shifts into silence and you go with her,

   Present till the last moment when dawn slips like a secret

   Into the garden, revealing and concealing everything.

41. In the silence that precedes dawn, a shock streams through,

   A pure beam that astounds all inner noise into light,

   An emptiness vaster than all the imagination.

   With day comes the illusions, the spells of memory,

   The suffering which was disclosed to the still mind,

   Now caught in the currents violent turning.

   Each moment is a dream in which we struggle to wake

To the here and now. Endless beginning and endless ending.

42. Flight to Bangalore

The city awaits like an imminent question, like a love and a danger

That beguiles the unquiet mind, threatening to uproot everything.

I bleed into the dawn, all of my past emptying like a bottomless dream.

The sun of a new world is rising, into which I cast everything.

1. I want to be in a place where I am able to live in the rush of experiencing, of doing, yet remaining in the silence of absorption and knowing simultaneously. I want to be a poet in action and in stillness, full in the movement of life, and full in the expression of rendering the eternal.

2. The fading blush blooms silence,

Our gaze drops as the streets vanish from outside our window.

The storm breathes inside of us, the torrents rush like towers

Collapsing from the sky, all the world around us narrowing

To a vague and dissonant shimmer, simmering on the emptiness

That will hold, then break between us.

The flowers burst like secret faces, unveiled in the quiet

Of our asylum from the mad, mad world.

The leaves on the trees turn, turning from heaven towards earth,

Heavy, sinking in the fragrance.

A soft wind settles, to sing the word we could not find,

To exclaim the expression we could not render,

Indeciphired or lost amongst all the names and places,

Buried somewhere amidst the tangled mire of our solitude,

Unquenched, sheltered, hidden from the self and the world.

3. Thoughts rush like masquerades bursting upon the tremulous mind.

A still voice quivers on the point between vision and void.

A door opens, a cry emerging from the dark, and I sink

Tunnelling, emptiness drawing me like a sword from the sheath

Of my past existence.

4. The road breaks and opens, before me a thousand turning faces

Dissolve in the stillness of your eyes. This silence is spinning me

To a single point, one note rising, to which all the rest will follow.

5. Hear me. Listen to my words tense and yearning,

Taut with the pull of your love. Listen to my hunger that beats

With caged wings against the infinity of your solitude.

Listen to my questions that hide and spring in shadow.

Listen to my silence, which goes out like a ship at dawn

To sink in the center of the sea, dissolving and absolving.

6. This silence drops like an anchor in my soul. The waves cease

Their continual rejoicing and lament. I cannot say where I am now,

Somewhere far, remote. My mind has flown like a dream half recalled,

Then forgotten. My words perish at the tip of their becoming.

I feel I am entering everything. I feel I am already nothing.

7. I want to dedicate my life to one thing in its entirety. To know what this is, it is essential that I enter completely into silence, and remain in this silence, until I emerge in perfect clarity and perfect confidence. I must attain a knowledge which will transcend every dream, every drama, every thrill, and every despair that the mind imposes on me. There is no way to truly enter this silence, until I accept that I am alone in the world. Only when I have fully understood and embraced what it is to be alone, can I begin to see God within me. And only when I have fully surrendered myself to that, can I fully love all others, remaining still in that silence.

8. In you I come back to my beginning, In you, my end.

In you I sink to cessation, in you I emerge to resound.

In your remembrance I am endless, even as I die again and again

Dreamt of in the dreams of my desires.

In you I am full in my emptiness, Empty in my fullness.

In you, there is no drawing nearer, no moving further away,

No turning, no looking, no going or staying.

In you everything is living as one, the myriad faces dissolve as a flood.

9. At the tip of the tongue I perish. I am what you cannot hold,

What you cannot grasp. I will go on without hope, without desire,

My past and my future are nobody, nowhere.

You will seek me and I will not come.

You will forget me and I will not go.

10. Silence engulfs the seas crash,

The moon rises solemn in the emptiness that follows,

In the hollows of my heart where it echoes, echoes.

The flowering bush fades,

I hide in the rocks high heaven,

Still amongst the death of my desires.

11. The current moves rapid upon the silence,

Rending with the tumult of an endless unlived dream.

In the eye of the storm, I sing, broken-hearted, free,

Empty, unseen.

12. What is poetry? Poetry is honouring the present, it is a state of being attuned to the inherent internal beauty that makes all outward manifestations possible. To live poetically is to live fearlessly. It is to be fully absorbed, while remaining fully detached from the subject of absorption. Living poetically is living clearly through intuition, as a heightened sensitivity and a higher expression of beauty are the same. A poem is a pure and condensed expression of reality. Likewise, a poet is a person who lives intensely, experiencing more from less, having extinguished all thoughts, feelings, and actions which carry any sense of halfheartedness.

13. Where is an end to desires? Where is an end to sorrow?

Observing everything, still I know nothing.

Where is the joy in the emptiness? Where is the answer in the pain?

How long must I lie here and wait?

14. Illusions claw at my eyes like a thousand fingers,

Tearing me, feasting on the perpetual weakness

That spins me day and night,

To a song that sends me sprawling,

To a dance that I cannot master,

In the stillness I shatter.

I cannot bear the transparency I ask for,

My mirror covers me like the abyss that I sought to escape,

Another hiding place amongst the books of dead saviours

That I keep shelved in hopes of resurrection.

I pick myself up like pieces of glass,

Like dreams that dance tenuously

Trembling to stand at the tip of their dissolution.

I hold myself prayerfully,

I cannot break again,

I cannot break again.

15. Open me up, empty me in your hands.

I am yours, I am yours.

Open me up, forgetting myself,

I am yours, I am yours.

I am the river in your blood,

I am the silence in your flood,

I am the void inside your voice,

I am the dream without a choice.

16. This black blood sinks like the humid haze of summer.

    All the days pass monotonous, married to the black scab

    Of this thickening monochrome. I choke on the endless wail

    Of the city's dank fumes, death sentences pour from the

    Ivory towers. The streets lose themselves in indifference,

    Fatigue runs like a river over the masses of faces,

    The faces hiding behind faces.

17. The night blackens in coils around me,

    The distances narrow to a single point in which I stand,

    Alone, a naked prisoner.

    I have nothing to say as the death rattles throng me.

    I have tasted them already, tired of the same haunt

    That comes again and again, the same vision that annihilates.

18. The hours pass slowly in the heavy hanging air,

    The crowds pass by slowly in the Suns scorching glare,

    The shadow trembles on the leaf

    And widens stair to stair,

    The noise inside the vacuum grows

    To split inside our ear.

    The passion dwindles slowly in the heavy hanging air,

    The emptiness inside us opens up to blankly stare,

The movements of our bodies fade

To shadows held in fear,

We crawl like insects on the wall

As silence draws us near.

The visions burn slowly in the heavy hanging air,

The past pleads with present

That the future should not hear,

The questions turn towards answers

That they will not dare to bear,

As the hours spin slowly in the heavy hanging air.

19. The inward ear stands steady, near,

The raindrops spread to cleanse and clear

From clouds dispersing trembling piers.

The heavens open, empty here,

They echo in my inward ear

All that's distant and all that's near

Gathers into one stillness here.

20. Bangalore monologues

A belt of fire scorches my waist, My heart stands stilled

In its tundra above the cauldron. Drums are beating monotonies

Through and through, dulling the inner monologue to a dumb drum.

My heart bursts inside its cage, freedom clawing at the periphery

That leads into the endless.

The light bursts, a bubble dissolving into its wake.

The barren dream unveils, opening its eye upon the rising horizon.

Above the surge and pull of the tide, it blinks, like a spirit caught

on the point of transmigration.

The tempo slows, dimming to a distant drawl in which I dance,

Self driven derelict cast out to float amongst the stars.

The night clutches me in its long train of impassible syllables,

The word descends from burning heights to sting its intractable query.

A cold wind drowns inside of me, namesake to a nameless dream.

I melt through the crowds, like the dying shouts that echo through runnels

to drift out emptied and far. The faces linger like a thickening cloud,

Into which I sink or swim, tearing, tearing at the veil between us.

Between the sound and the silence a small hope flutters

And catches hold, gnawing at the hole inside of me,

Where the gods stand in silent procession

Burning and burning towards their illumination.

My cry springs up like a flock fleeing to beat time to the horizon.

The flush of summer draws to slow disclosures,

A cold wind snaps like a seam that bursts free,

Freeing me to the solitude that reaches further and further.

I am remote, an uncharted mark spreading slowly through the universe.

I have touched the edge of what I cannot know,

It plagues me, persistently knowing.

I sail through the silence, a fleet weaving white sails

To the limitless sky. From the bottom of the oceans floor

A thought rises, writhing from a deeper silence.

The tide turns calamitous, pushing the prow to panic.

On the perilous point I spin, pinned to a dream drowning silence.

The pillowy plunge draws to a close desperate arguments

Of the feverish cry, the mind strikes a tangled root upon

The bed of flowers, the red hot tongue drips in its lonely fury.

In the shallow contrivings of my breath, this room widens

And narrows upwards, spinning into the eye of the sky,

A single spoke in which my other self is dancing,

Dancing freely, freely.

All the colors bleed into an abyss of monochrome,

Into a center in which I am spiralling through the rungs of hell,

Searching for a hook on which to pin my ruinous self,

But in vain, in vain. I sink, my dreams floating out

Around me like the clear bells of dawn.

Morning breaks and flows in ripples, the wind passes

Sighing the passing of time. I am waking in the cry of dispersion,

The long train of night has hauled me through all the editions

And revisions and submissions of a boundless tormented mind.

From an impenetrable center I spiral emptied out,

A loose thread spinning on the edge of a deafening nightfall.

The stars beam and tremble like hallucinations,

Burning me in the omniscient gaze of their turning.

21. LASIK

The light dances in leaps and spirals

Tunnels of white spinning higher and higher

In the lengthening eye of the cylinder.

Under the microscope the cornea burns,

Blinking to escape the flash that floods everything.

The voices of the nurses echo in the chamber,

Falling one after the other like leaves drifting

And spreading to submerge the empty halls.

Like paper lamps floating over the black and moonless night,

They breathe the softness of a moth like dreaming.

The hands of the doctor move seamlessly in deft precision,

Through an endless stream, a glass reflecting water.

A flick and the outside light pours back from the cylinder

Revolving in its long black void.

The goggles peel back, the room widens into view,

And I rise reluctant.

22. Vipassana

As the gaze drops inward the worlds begin to dissolve,

Time unravelling the thread of its existence.

A trapdoor flies open, baring the soul as it surges up

From infirmity into the clear light of the ever open eye.

23. Madanapalle

Housewives line the balconies like dreams displayed before a dying love.

The wind lulls to a deafening drawl, the last sunbeam strikes like

A broken chord through this monotony of madness.

The stones on the street echo, a grief bound cry dancing

From light to light, night to night.

The curtains fly while the wind sings sorrow

The day lengthens in the wake of its toil

The shadow heaves a sigh as the house grows dim

The leaves hang gilded in the silence and the sin.

The door stands open as the clouds are passing over

The coils burn like lovers trapped in secrecy of cover

The end of day is drawing like the last unsaid farewell

My words are only cracks that line the mirror on the shelf.

The masjid's call to prayer echoes black inside my brain

The women stand like statues clad in hopes and useless shame

The unwed girls comb their hair in dreams of matrimony's gain

While the married women mourn their loss, hanging laundry on the gates.

The children run from stairs to street, and back again and again,

The light in their eyes is the only thing shining through all of the pain.

Eid Mubarak

The women emerge in their colors, the men have all gone out to pray,

Mornings solemnity passes into flames of the blistering day.

The guests arrive shedding their sadness, greetings dispel dark days past,

The house opens up like a story as the wind carries seeds of the fast.

The cooks trundle barrels of onions, scents rise and curl up the spires

Of the masjid that stands in the splendor and darkness that history transpires.

24. Drifting down from tangled heights, resolve strikes at the root,

   An all resounding chord that breaks past and future.

   A symphony plays begins the dividing mind

   Where all madness is stilled for a moment,

   Where time cracks open to shatter all the things

   That were seen and unseen.

25. Unable to perfect, unable to move smoothly with time's pull and passage,

I dream in broken sequences, neither here nor there

But in some still and starry heaven where the faces of the poets

And the saints beam in their endless profusion.

I have tried and I have tried, but the shadow that falls each night

Still drags me to the edge, where I burn in the abyss of fear and memory.

26. The street ends where the sun drips gold

The evening gathers in darkening folds,

The emptiness pushes me inward to spin

In the eye of a needle where all dreams fall in.

How will I pass through the mires of time

Echoing past, future, and mind?

Every thought building a new paradigm

Into endless creation and endless dying.

Dreaming the sun was rising again

I woke on the edge of a burning lens

That dissolved into sight as the light could not end,

And has left me since wondering where I have been.

27. The twilight of our dreaming descends,

A silence slips to sound infinity through the emptiness,

Where insatiable illusions are echoing to the end.

Stillness mirrors the unshakable self as it sings

the calamity of every hour, sinking, leaping,

Beaming into embrace of death or dissolution.

The twilight of our dreaming ascends,

We emerge in the golden orbs of our desire,

Yearning to touch and eclipse the fire

That Burns through every hour.

Our silence is a dark and fragrant flower

That drifts down like snow over all the mire,

Over all the ache that opens into streams of ice and fire.

The channels of our separate selves respire,

Restlessness and rest entire,

Revolve the sacral spheres.

Returning back from India

28. Memories stir in the shadows flung by the vines

Over the darkening window, awakening into visions

And revisions of past and future, the bound soul

Is caught unbinding through circuits of transmigration.

A cold wind whorls dry the sap of summer,

The fruits lie buried sunken in the leaves,

Rotting slowly in the covering darkness,

Slumbering, slumbering.

How we are slumbering till something shakes us,

Deep in the roots a far cry echoes upward,

A current of light opening from a narrow shaft

That widens and widens into rivers,

Multitudes of rivers converging on the single point

In which I dream, dream, wake and dream.

29. The fields sleep a deep dreamless sleep

With no voice and no turning.

All around the world stirs,

Clocks turning in the dark,

In the spell of voice and dreaming.

The wind lulls, opening a space, a breath spanning

All that is between thought and no thought,

Between feeling and no feeling,

Between fullness and void.

The wind lays waste to the still plains

That still echo, uttering stillness.

Dark pines emerge on the horizon,

Shadows amassing shadows on the edge of stillness.

The land empties, the vast spaces sink, deepening

Dreaming on the edge of stillness.

30. The mountain is sinking into the valley,

    Filled with the emptiness of sky.

    The moon hides herself within the emptiness,

    Unreached and unreaching.

    Our song sinks into the dream in the darkness.

31. Silence preceding and silence following,

    The thick knot that stretches and groans after the expanse of love,

    the emptiness echoing before, after, and now,

    a perpetual tolling that follows us into the darkness

    In which we would forget everything, lose everything,

    Were it not for the seeker, intent, still clinging to the knot of desire,

    Still bound within the myriad faces of hatred and love,

    These chimeras of the fire that leap and spiral

    Back to the depths of oblivion.

    Silence preceding and silence following.

    Remembrance after remembrance,

    The knot cracks but will not sunder,

    The mind sways but will not stay,

    Fearful of the outcome or cessation of action,

    The will fixes itself unmoving in the movement towards restoration,

    It's last cry of "I, I, I" at last sinking into the silence.

32. From the ground of sorrow I emerge, a dark dream,

   Heavy, wet, dripping with the longing of love,

   A hopeless embrace that sinks everything to return

   Back to the void from which it proceeded.

   The rain rushes in currents, the torrents pool inside of me,

   A savage windbeaten song rushing to merge back

   Into the ground of its being. The ocean swells inside of me,

   Uncontained, I am uncontaining.

33. Entering the stillness, blunting the sharp edge of the chaos

   In which the mind spins, a lost surveyor is stretched to the millionth star.

   In purgatory, dreaming of the worlds past and the worlds to come,

   Traversing the immeasurable spaces between the mines of time,

   The mind fixed in time, ceaselessly strives to be freed from time.

   Infinity haunts the line of the sinking horizon,

   Diminishing to return, returning to diminish,

   The passions and the grief of time.

34. Cut all the ties, break all the bonds.

   The self alone knows the way home.

   Only the empty hands can open,

   Only the silent eyes can see.

   Best heard is the song that does not rise, does not descend,

   But hums endless through the dark and light,

Fixed in the void amongst the worlds changing harmonies.

35. In all the stories of my life, there are only a couple main characters, a couple threads intersecting, or not intersecting, but sort of parallel. Yet there is a very deep conflict between them, a friction that is almost crushing, that is coming close to madness. The two intersecting threads unravel into something that feels like a million threads, an overwhelming cacophony in such a small space, in something that is looking from the outside like almost nothing.

I do not even want to be the protagonist in a story. I want to dissolve into nothing, I want to swallow all the stories, all the characters, so that there is nothing left to act, so there is no desire left to keep the protagonist going. There is only the spirit, no time or place. I will not be bound in any time or place. But I am acting from a time and place, all the while dreaming that I am not in that time or place. I am in this world, but there is something that will not allow me to be fully here, something continually pushing me to the edge of an abyss, which I cannot fathom, but which I long to perish into. It is a space that I know, but cannot name. All the stories of my life melt away on this edge, and I want to leap, leaving everything, every thought, every feeling, every memory, every face, but I cannot. I am sucked back into this world, and I am trying to live as all the people around me seem to be living, but there is an inexpressible pain, an inexpressible longing, sometimes an inexpressible bliss, because I have just touched, but cannot enter that place.

36. Purity burns the root from which the inexhaustible axes spin,

These thousand headed demons sprung from a thousand thirsting dreams,

Unseen and unreconciled to the desiring mind.

I run after these, mad with the cry of "I, I, I".

I drown in the cry of I, oceans spill from the wound that is I,

Time in I, life in I, death in I. Purity burns the root,

Through heart and mind, to sight. The thoughtless eye is light,

There- gone am I.

37. Dengue Fever

I am vomiting up the world into my mouth,

I am trying to vomit love and everything it entails

I am trying to vomit the poison of passion

The thousand petalled elixir of death that squeezes out my soul,

The million roots entangled in the bottomless black, sinking

Deeper, deeper into the ground of which there is no fathoming,

No sound, no sight, no recollection of the things I had sought to master,

No remedy for the raving of the soul, no quiet

For the endless surge of this furious purging ocean.

I am vomiting up the world into my mouth,

I am the earth and the earth is swallowing me

I am the mother trying to rebirth herself

I am the child of a million races

I am the secret of a million forms

I am trying to vomit everything that memory taught me,

I am trying to vomit all the visions of the future,

I am trying to vomit humanity, rising, sinking,

Churning inside of me.

I am trying to vomit the self, all the duplicities of the self,

Dividing and multiplying through the universe,

Through the mind, through the heart,

Through the body, trying to vomit itself.

Love and dreams are two parenthesis.

Between them I place my body

And discover the world." ~Adonis

Between your body and my body

I was writing parenthesis,

Leaving the space between them

Open for the world to manifest

Itself in wonder.

Between your body and my body

I walked a desert,

Burning like a star fallen

On an empty page

Of unwritten parenthesis,

The wind writing and erasing

Your name across my eyebrows,

The sun burning a hole through my heart

Like a coin of immeasurable value.

Between your body and my body

I drank the mirage of desire

Haunting me into the dark well

That sprang between hands of silence,

Haunting me into the resounding gong

Of my own reflections

Where I searched self after self,

This world unfolding.

Between your body and my body

I heard from afar

The ring of a circling emptiness,

Spinning us like dreams

Playing on the fingertip

Of a god.

2. Wilderness of Meaning

The world is a wilderness of meaning

And I am a lover travelling

In the wilderness of being.

This is not a story about keeping,

This is a story about seeing,

And about how we become

All the things that we see.

This world is a wilderness of meaning

And I am a lover drinking

In everything I see.

I am the drop sinking

To every rivers stream,

I am the bush fading

In the sunlight's harshest beam.

I am the flower that blooms

To perish in this wilderness of meaning.

The world is a wilderness of meaning

And I am a lover teeming

With every sound I hear.

I am the thunder sleeping

Before the lids of leaping,

Lighting burning clear.

I am the rains arriving

Upon the winds deep sighing,

Turning distance near.

The world is a world of wilderness of meaning

And I am a lover seeing

How meaning turns to face

The abyss that rocks the dreaming

In skies past reach of keeping,

Where meanings change their place.

The world is a wilderness of meaning

That has held me in my being

And left me with no trace

Of what I used to carry,

Of what I kept to bury

In places changing place.

The world is a wilderness of meaning

Where all that I see seeming

Is not what I could make.

I crack inside the sleeping

Of what I once was keeping,

To open world's embrace.

The meaning of this being

I fashion as I'm seeing

The faces changing face.

3. Dancing Venus

Dancing in the deep blue,

I watched the morning star rise

Like a sacred word beaming

Through a wilderness of darkness.

On my tongue moonbeams spun

Webs of the finest threads,

To catch the sacred words

Sweet falling.

As I was falling

I saw moonbeams rise to catch me,

Drenched me in the starlit

Sound of silence.

Dancing in the deep blue,

The morning star surprised me

Slipped veils from inside me

To open face to face.

Within the webs still shining

We're sacred words untying,

Dissolving back to space.

Dancing in the deep blue,

The morning star looked, rising

Within her own abiding,

The peace of sacred sound.

She smiled the world sleeping,

Lifted the lids of dreaming

To nectar flowing down,

To floods of silence slipping

Sipping sacred sound.

4.

When the lid of night closes over our eyes

And our contemplations of love settle

Moving from thought to stillness,

The moon turns her face shining upon us

And lets us laugh as god and goddess,

Tasting and washing away the brilliant

And dreaded stains of illusion.

When the lid of night closes over our eyes

And we burn through the ache of lovers

Into the clear reflection of awareness,

Passion turns to stillness

Bestowing bliss in the contemplation of love.

When the lid of night closes over our eyes

And we drink the nectar of the moon within us,

The darkness is lit shining

Giving thought away to silence.

When the lid of night closes over our eyes

We travel the dream moving through every river,

Becoming the first drop of the first ripple

Beheld in the contemplation of love.

5.

Between your voice and my voice I walked the path

Of the sun rising to meet me.

In the early morning light, the birds sang through

Webs of grey shadow catching dewdrops,

Glistening like crystals upon eyes first opening.

The wind rising to move through the grass at dawn

Was the unspeakable voice touching everything

In the gesture of blessing.

Between your voice and my voice I saw

All the earth reflected in the dome of the sky.

Our bodies became the mirrors of the cosmic One,

Entrancing and enchanting between our voices

The power of blessing.

In the early morning light I saw moons fade

In the rising run coming to burn on our tongue

The unspeakable ways speaking blessing.

6.

Like perfume poured out

Surrounding me with kisses,

The thought of you fills me awake

Every night as I turn in my bed

To touch the veil that slips

Like a satin sheet between us.

Your memory is like the end of songs,

Falling like water from the moon

Into wells of sweet silence,

Where I drink the streams

Of the dawns contemplation.

Like perfume poured out

You fill me with your kisses,

Awakening me in the flowers of dawn.

Your breathe is the envelope of night

Keeping me as I come to breathe you.

Your gaze is the like the end of songs

Fixed like a stream always flowing

Holding and upholding me,

Arriving at the door of each moment.

Like perfume poured out

You remain as an invisible wholeness,

Awake in the night and the day

Where I wait for you,

My eyes at rest in your kisses.

7.

Lightning Source UK Ltd.
Milton Keynes UK
UKHW050633260922
409457UK00008B/617

9 789356 649934